Puppy Training: The Complete Guide

How to Train and Housebreak your Puppy into an Obedient and Well Behaved Member of the Family

Table of Contents

Introduction 3

Chapter 1: Understanding Puppies 5

Chapter 2: General Tips and Info Before Training
              Your Puppy 10

Chapter 3: What you need for your Puppy and Why 15

Chapter 4: Housebreaking your Puppy 22

Chapter 5: Puppy Training for Toileting Outside 26

Chapter 6: Clicker Training 29

Chapter 7: Crate Training 34

Chapter 8: How to Walk Your Puppy 40

Chapter 9: Jumping and Biting 50

Conclusion 58

Introduction

Every species, human or not, has to go through a period of training. If you think about it, humans have one of the longest training periods of any species because it takes us years to learn how to talk, walk, run, jump, and learn the millions of facts we are taught in school. As young children, we repeat many of the things we are learning to cement them to memory. Our parents are consistent, patient, and considerate in teaching us about morals, ethics, values, safety, and all the other things we have to learn.

So why would it be different for a young puppy, a few weeks old? Your puppy has to go through a learning process. The more consistent, patient, and consideration you show your puppy, the easier it will be for him/her to learn what is expected of him.

As puppy owners, we can forget these concepts. We can forget, in our busy lives, what it truly took for us to learn all that we did to become intelligent, responsible adults.

It might be easier for you to learn how to train your puppy, by thinking along the lines of how long it took you as a child to be obedient and well behaved. It is why numerous puppy training books often mention over and over that you need to be considerate, consistent, and patient with your puppy. Now that you have been reminded, you can go on to learn the truly important aspects of training.

The chapters of this book will focus on:

- Understanding your puppy's behavior
- General tips to help you prior to bringing your puppy home
- What you need to buy for your puppy
- Housebreaking Tips
- Toilet training for outside
- Clicker training
- Crate training
- How to walk your puppy
- How to curb jumping and biting behaviors

You are in a learning process, just as your dog is. You are more than welcome to make mistakes, as you know your puppy will. The key is to keep a positive attitude, stick with the training, and remember that you can train your puppy.

Chapter 1: Understanding Puppies

Animal behaviorists study the psychology (behaviors) of animals, such as dogs. Through their work, we have a better understanding of puppy behavior. Your puppy lacks vocal cords. While, he/she can make sounds, he/she is unable to tell you how they feel, what they want, and it is your job to read their behavior. You also need to understand the character traits, and tendencies your puppy breed is known for.

Puppy Psychology

Puppies are infants that will grow at a quick rate. They will be born with certain instincts and then it is your job to teach your puppy what he/she needs to know. The puppy's mother uses imprinting, such as requesting the puppy to sniff a smell and providing a stimulus to show whether that smell is good or bad. You can do the same. The training techniques in later chapters will ask you to provide a stimulus and teach your puppy a behavior. Learning will be through habituation (repetition), associative learning, and imitation.

Imitation is fairly easy to understand. If you bark, your dog will bark.

If you turn off the TV at night, call your puppy, and go to bed soon you will find all you have to do is turn off the TV and go to bed. Your puppy will learn that the TV off at night means bed. Through habituation, your puppy knows the routine.

Associative learning is a process where you introduce a stimulus and request a new response. Pavlov's dogs are an example of associative learning. He taught dogs to salivate to a noise versus food. At first he would introduce meat powder into the controlled environment with the dogs. Soon the dogs started salivating before the meat powder was distributed. He then took the meat powder and a ringing bell, where he predicted the dogs would soon start to salivate when the bell rang, without meat powder being distributed. He was correct. The bell became a neutral stimulus and the meat powder was the unconditioned stimulus. The study aimed to show that a stimulus would elicit a response from the dog and that one could train a certain behavior. Most of what your dog learns will be through associative learning because you will provide a stimulus, ask for a certain response, and reward your puppy.

To train your puppy, you will need to provide a motivational reason or reward. Puppies are motivated by their instincts to have food, water, shelter, and love. Your puppy is going to want to have action in their lives. They will also have needs and desires.

Your goal is to meet the needs, desires, and teach appropriate actions, while ignoring the inappropriate behavior. Consider a toddler for a moment. A toddler will learn that negative responses from you get them attention. For example, if they throw a toy on the ground when you are talking and you pick it up, the child will throw the toy again if they want you to pay attention to them.

Puppies will do the same thing. They can develop negative behaviors simply because you provided a response to it. Even a "no" is better than being ignored in a puppy's mind.

Your puppy has emotions. They can be sad, happy, depressed, bored, worried, or fearful. A puppy's vocalizations and body language are two ways you can determine what your puppy is feeling. Their actions are another. A protective puppy will stand in front of you and defend you. A confused puppy may lay his/her ears back, tilt their head, and look at you with those soulful eyes.

Stages of Puppyhood

Puppies need their mothers from 0 to 2 weeks. During weeks 2 to 4, there is a transitional period, where the puppy is starting to eat puppy food versus milk, and they are eventually able to leave their mother and be with their owner. Between 4 and 12 weeks is the socialization period of your puppy, where he/she needs to meet other dogs, people, and learn how to interact. If you have other pets in the home, 3 to 6 months is going to be a ranking period. It is a time where your puppy will learn its position in the household. If your puppy has a dominant personality, he/she will try to establish their alpha ranking. Puppies are adolescence starting about 6 months to 18 months. Depending on the breed, your puppy can reach adulthood at one or two years.

Character Traits

Your puppies character or personality traits will start to develop at seven weeks. Their full personality will be evident by 10 to 12 weeks. To choose the right puppy, it is best to wait for week 7. Start to visit your puppy and at week 10 to 12 evaluate your puppy's personality again. The environment your puppy is in will also determine the character traits you see. Your dog may act completely different in their home turf versus in a new home.

Genetics is going to factor in with regards to personality. Since this is not a book listing all dog breeds and traits, it is in your best interest to get a book on the dog breeds you are most interested in and learn about their genetic predispositions.

Non-genetic character traits are something you will need to observe. These traits will develop based on your care, love, and how you meet their needs. A puppy can also have different personality traits around different people because they understand what is or is not acceptable.

For instance, a dog might go to work with its owner for several months. The dog is then left at home with another person. The new person ignores the dog, works, and provides a stable play routine. The dog learns to sleep, play on their own, and ask to go to the bathroom. However, when the dog goes back to work he doesn't associate this same behavior. Instead, he is rambunctious, gets into everything and demands attention. It is because the owner is now seen as a play partner. The owner comes home and plays with the dog, so now the dog thinks play time is whenever the owner is with him. He/she starts to show that he/she isn't going to listen because he/she wants to play. He/she tries to assert dominance over the owner to get what he/she wants.

Tendencies

Tendencies are typical puppy behaviors seen in breeds. For example, scent hounds have medium energy levels, they are easily distracted, and are very social animals. As you read about your puppy's breed, you will find a list of certain tendencies, which will help you determine how to train your puppy.

Cool Facts:

- Approximately five to 30 minutes after your puppy eats, your puppy will need to go to the bathroom, most often defecating.

- For each month of age, your puppy can hold their bladder approximately one hour. This means an eight-month old puppy should be able to hold his/her bladder for eight hours.

- Goldsmiths College, located in London, has shown that dogs feel empathy for owners and strangers.

- The University of Vienna determined dogs understand when they are being mistreated.

- Dogs have more olfactory receptors than humans, thus they have a heightened sense of smell, which you can use in training.

- Max Planck taught a border collie 200 vocabulary words. It shows your dog can learn words, their names, and commands through proper training.

Chapter 2: General Tips and Info Before Training Your Puppy

What would happen in your working life if you provided a report one time with no errors, but the next time there were errors and you continued to have an inconsistent pattern? How did you learn how to type on a keyboard with accuracy? As a child, when you were instructed to do something, such as "please, clear the table" and you didn't do it, what happened? What happens when someone asks you to do something, but you don't understand their words because the phone bleeped out? How do you feel when you get reprimanded versus rewarded at work?

- For inconsistency, you probably get retraining and told that after a certain period of time, without improvement you will lose your job.

- Learning to type you had to repeatedly practice.

- If you did not do as asked, you were disciplined, and requested to follow the request.

- If a statement is unclear, you ask the person to repeat and then follow the request.

- When you are given rewards you feel 100% better than when you are reprimanded. You might also feel embarrassed due to the reprimand or feel it was unjustified.

The best tip that can be offered to you—is to think about your puppy like you do other humans. Your puppy has emotions, but needs time to learn. You are given chances to be consistent, repeat, and follow requests. Your dog has to be given the same consideration.

Consistency

To obtain consistency from your puppy, you must first be disciplined enough to provide the same consistency. If you work for one hour on the sit command and then go three weeks before you work for another hour on the same command, your dog will have forgotten everything they learned the first time. Providing a routine for your puppy is how they learn.

It is not just about training commands, toileting, and other aspects. Consistency is about the routine you provide for your puppy. Each day you get up at a certain time, your puppy gets up with you. What happens during that day?

Sample Routine:

1. Your puppy gets up
2. You let your puppy relieve himself/herself because it was a long night of sleeping
3. You feed your puppy at the same time each day
4. You prepare for work, and your puppy prepares for the day alone or perhaps with you
5. You come home, let your puppy out, give him/her lunch
6. You go back to work, and your puppy goes back to their daily routine of being alone

7. After work, you come home to let your puppy out, feed him/her

8. After your dinner, it is time for puppy play

Of course, somewhere in your busy daily routine, you have to train. Your puppy is going to listen better if he/she is not fully energized after a boring day. You do not want your puppy tired either, but you do want some of the energy to be run or played out.

Make sure you are consistent with the routine and training each day.

Repetition

Repetition is not only done through consistency, but also in those training periods. You got your dog to sit after giving him/her a treat. Now, you will repeat the process. On the third attempt, you ask your dog to sit, but give him a different type of reward.

If your dog is not listening to the request or does not understand you, repeat the voice command once. Guide your puppy to show them the behavior you want. Ask your puppy for the behavior. When your puppy provides that behavior, give a reward, and repeat the command, until your puppy is no longer confused.

Voice Commands

A common mistake among dog owners and voice commands, is too many words. Your dog can understand one word and associate it with a behavior. Through repetition, you can give one command, praise, and follow it with a second command, such as sit and stay.

First your puppy has to learn to sit. After sit is known and always followed, then you can start training stay. Eventually, your puppy can learn a string of commands, but always start with simple, one word commands.

Rewarding

Rewards need to vary. If you give your dog a treat every time they follow a voice command, you are simply teaching your puppy that for the stimulus they need to provide a response and it will always be food. If they do not get food, then they will refuse the command. By rubbing down your puppy, saying good, or giving a treat, your puppy learns that he/she gets something it wants, but it will not always be food.

For example, if your puppy jumps up and down at the door, you can tell your puppy to sit. When the puppy sits and stays, then you open the door and reward them with what they already wanted.

Your Mindset

Your mindset is just as important. If you lack patience you will have a tendency to yell, threaten, or physically punish your puppy. All of these are horrible because your puppy just lacks training and understanding. You are your puppy's parent. You are responsible for keeping your emotional control and the appropriate patience.

If you cannot, then sit quietly. Be calm in your body language and facial expressions. Wait for your inner self to calm down, and start over. Your puppy can read your body language and facial expressions, just as much as the tone of your voice.

Have you ever noticed a dog tuck his tail and lay his ears back, when someone yells, but is not yelling at the dog? It is a natural instinct to tuck in, and feel empathy for another person.

As long as you can remember that your puppy is like a child and that consistency, patience, voice commands, repetition, and rewards all help you train him/her, you will succeed.

Chapter 3: What you need for your Puppy and Why

Your puppy is dependent on you to provide them with food, water, shelter and entertainment. To make their lives happy and fun, you will need to buy a few things prior to bringing your puppy home.

Food/water Bowls:

It goes without saying that your puppy needs something to eat and drink from. You will see all types of puppy bowls at the store, but which ones will you buy? To avoid spending more money as your puppy grows, choose a bowl size that will fit your full grown puppy's head. Your puppy prefers a larger bowl size than its head, so they can see while eating. Smaller dogs can use smaller bowls for food.

For water, you want something that will be able to keep plenty of water. You do need to replace the water, frequently, if you go with a regular bowl. Your puppy like's fresh water, just like you.

The best option for water, is to have a fountain style, where your puppy can get fresh water, cycled through the device. You want a fairly large water container, with a bowl that will fit their head. Again, it is about being able to see, while getting a drink. Puppies have instincts to protect themselves. As wild dogs, prior to domestication, dogs had to be wary of sounds and movement, thus they are still very alert when they get a drink.

Grooming Kit:

Like all puppy items, there will be choices in grooming kits. If you have a short haired puppy, then a brush, toothbrush and paste, and nail clippers may be all you need. If you intend on paying a vet for teeth cleaning six months, you still need a toothbrush and paste, so your dog is trained to sit through the procedure. In fact, you should brush your dog's teeth regularly.

Other grooming kits have scissors and hair grooming tools. Again, this is something you can pay to have done, if you do not feel you will be able to keep your dog looking beautiful.

Dog shampoo is an essential part of the grooming kit too, unless you will take your dog to a groomer every week. During the warmer months, you definitely need to ensure your dog gets a bath on a weekly basis to check for ticks, fleas, and other bugs. Your shampoo is not designed to be animal safe, although it may be. Additionally, there are some fragrances that could actually harm your puppy's skin. For this reason, buying a dog approved shampoo is best.

Chewable Toys:

Puppies are destructive. Rubber toys like rubber chickens can be torn into small pieces and consumed with ease. Puppies do not understand that it is dangerous for them. Even a tennis ball can be completely destroyed by your puppy in minutes, when he/she wants to chew. You need to provide toys that can be chewed. Nyla bones are very popular because they are hard and not easy to damage. They also help keep the back teeth clean. The downside is the noise they create, which can be annoying to you.

It used to be acceptable to provide bones to puppies, but now it is thought that the bones when torn apart can actually cut your puppy internally because of the sharp edges.

A good compromise is the greenie treats. These treats can be chewed. It takes time to chew pieces off, but at least it will not harm your pet. Most greenies are also designed with teeth cleaning properties.

Kongs are another chew toy, where you can put peanut butter or treats inside. Your dog works to get the reward, but also has a hardier toy that will not break when chewed.

Play Toys:

Tennis balls or other balls, ropes, stuffed animals with squeaky properties, rubber chickens, and a number of other toys sold can be used during play. These are the toys you play tug of war with or teach your dog to drop, so you can throw it and they can retrieve it. These toys do not have to be hardy for chewing because you will take them away after play is over.

By training your dog to know they have certain chew toys and play toys, they will understand when you trade one for the other. For example, it is late, you want to sit, and you do not want to play. If you take the play toy away and provide a chew toy, your dog will learn to understand that it is time to chew and play on their own.

Stair Gates:

If you have stairs in your home, you may want to invest in some stair gates. Even door gates can be useful. You may want your puppy to stay out of certain rooms, when you are not with them. Stair gates and door gates will help you with this. Of course, you can close the doors, but if you have cats that may be locked in the room without a litter box, it is not an option.

A gate is something that tells your puppy they are not allowed to go there. You may need to work on training larger dogs not to jump the gates, but typically, they will understand that they are prevented from going in or out. It may also be a safety measure.

Puppies can find anything a toy. They might go into a bathroom and find the toilet paper. Your puppy might find a Kleenex box to destroy. It is harmful for this paper to be consumed. By stopping your puppy from going certain places, you prevent them from encountering a dangerous situation.

ID Tags:

Any time you go out, your dog needs their ID tags. If you want to make a special tag in a machine, you can. You can also use the ID tag the puppy breeder or humane society gave you. It needs to have the dog's name, puppy ID numbers, shot details, and your address/phone number. The ID tag should be used to tell someone that your dog is safe because it has had its vaccines, its name so they can call him/her, and how to locate the owner. ID chips are also an option. Your pet can get a chip implant that is read by a special device. Vets and shelters have these devices, helping pets get back to their owners.

Dog Bed:

A dog bed can be used for two things. It can be the place your puppy knows they are going to sleep every night. It can also be a place to take naps. You will determine if you want to set the precedent of your puppy sleeping in the same bed with you.

After inviting your dog onto your bed at night, you will not be able to train him/her to sleep in its bed at night.

Dog beds, are generally cup shaped, with a high back on one side. Your dog is able to curl up or stretch its legs out. It always depends on the type of puppy, but most often larger dogs like to stretch out with their legs out in front, and their back against something.

When buying a bed, it should be large enough for your puppy. Remember that puppies will grow, so a larger bed, about the size that will fit their full grown size is best.

It is also a good idea to get one with a washable cover, in the event of accidents. Puppies do not like toe pee or defecate in the same area they sleep, but accidents happen. Furthermore, if you have other pets like cats, the bed could be an invitation to the toilet instead of a dirty litter box.

Dog Crate:

A dog crate is a place for your animal to feel comfortable, not punished. It is understandable that during the day, you will want your puppy to be in a safe place. You do not want your puppy to be free to chew on the furniture, blankets, shoes, coats, clothing, or papers that might be spread around your home. Puppies will find anything to play with when bored.

But, you want your puppy to be comfortable in their crate. The crate needs to be an appropriate size for your growing puppy. This means your puppy has room to lay down, spread out, and not run into their food and water.

Most crates are made with a plastic, removable bottom for accidental toileting issues. The rest of the crate are either plastic or metal. Metal crates, where your puppy can see out are usually more comfortable. The plastic crate usually has a few places to see out, but it is more for air than for comfort.

Harness and Leash:

Various collars and harnesses are sold. Some collars go around the puppy's legs, so if they try to run or get out of control, their legs will fold. Collars are simple devices, usually made of nylon that go around the neck. It is something your dog might be able to pull his/her head out of.

For walks, you want a harness that your puppy cannot wriggle out of. Harnesses made for walking go around the neck, along the front of their chest, and around their legs, under their bellies. It also allows the leash to be attached on the back, to avoid tripping your puppy with the leash.

Leashes come in one length and retractable types. A retractable leash allows your puppy to walk ahead of you, but be reeled back in when you need him/her closer. With a one length sized, leash, you can still bring your dog closer, but you must do so by hand. They also have a set limit on how far they can be away from you.

Most towns/cities/states have leash laws, where you must have your puppy on a leash in public areas. If you go to a dog park, you can usually remove the leash. When you walk in nature on your own property, your puppy can walk beside you without a leash. However, it is also a good idea to teach your puppy how to withstand the restraint of the harness and leash, so he/she is comfortable with it at all times.

Chapter 4: Housebreaking your Puppy

Housebreaking your puppy can seem like a monumental job. It does take quite a bit to teach your puppy that it is okay to toilet in the house, but it must be a specific location.

Puppy Pads are great for housebreaking your puppy. If you intend on letting your puppy toilet in the house, you want to make certain it is not on the carpet or hardwood floor. You also want to provide a place he/she can relieve themselves throughout the day that is not their bed.

Your puppy does not want to be in a crate with defecation and pee, while also having to sleep there. If you have a puppy breed, you can trust not to chew the entire house apart in boredom, then housebreak your puppy.

Lay out a clear place, using puppy pads. A puppy pad may have an odor. Many have a fragrance to avoid the ammonia smell in the home. If your puppy does not go on the pad even after training, consider that it might be the smell of the pad that makes it the wrong place for your puppy.

After all, what smells great to you, may truly irritate your dog's sense of smell.

Step by Step on How to Housetrain your Puppy

1. Clear out a room you are not using.
2. Put plastic over the entire floor.

3. Cover it with newspaper.

4. Place two or three puppy pads in the room.

5. Place a puppy bed or crate for sleeping in the room.

6. Give your puppy food and water.

7. When your puppy indicates a need to relieve itself, carry him/her to the puppy pad.

8. If your dog tries to walk away or sniff another area, gently, and calmly, place your puppy back on the pad.

9. When your puppy goes on the pad, immediately provide a treat.

10. Repeat this process.

What to do when your dog doesn't listen

You are bound to have some issues with housetraining your puppy. Simply showing your puppy the right pad and providing a treat, will not always do.

Your puppy may forget. He/she may wait too long. They may realize during the day they do not get treats and you are not there to stop them.

The good news is—you can get your puppy to go in the right place.

Leave a soiled pad in the room. It should be free of poo, but have a little ammonia smell to it. If you do not have a soiled pad, take a Q-tip outside with you the next time you take your puppy out. Swipe a bit of the urine from this bathroom break. Rub the Q-tip on the pad.

The scent will help your puppy investigate and find the right place to go to the bathroom.

Never yell at your puppy or make him/her feel embarrassed or ashamed.

Always pick up your puppy and bring him/her to the pad when you catch the puppy going in an improper place.

Also remember that the age of your puppy determines how frequently they need to go, as well as their size. If you know when your puppy went last, then you can time when they will need to go again.

This way, you are on hand to help your puppy find the right location.

Clean up the wrongly soiled location. Use a pet cleaner, so the odor is completely removed.

Always praise or give treats when your puppy goes in the right location.

Eventually, you can use voice or clicker commands to help your puppy find the right place to toilet.

Make sure you provide a clean pad for your puppy in the same place, every time.

Bathroom Accidents due to Excitement

Housetraining has another side to it. There are times when your puppy is so young that excitement can cause him/her to go to the bathroom without meaning to do so.

If this happens, quickly bring your excited puppy to the area in the house they should go.

Your puppy can finish his/her business needs. You can also open the door and let your puppy go outside if an accident occurs.

Quietly and calmly clean up the mess. Do not yell. Do not say "bad dog." Just clean it up.

The next time your puppy goes reward him/her.

If your puppy is excited and holds his/her bladder, give him a treat.

Chapter 5: Puppy Training for Toileting Outside

The fact states, your puppy for every month of life can hold their bladder an hour each. A puppy who is just four weeks, needs to be let outside nearly every hour. As the owner and the human, it is your responsibility to ensure your puppy is let outside or housetrained. You cannot get angry at your puppy because he/she pees or poops in the wrong location, or any inside location, if you make him/her hold their needs.

It would be like asking a newly potty trained child to hold it because you don't want to go into a bathroom right now.

Choose the Rules

It is also your responsibility to choose the rules of where your puppy is allowed to pee and defecate. If you have a large outside space and do not care if he/she goes anywhere that is fine. However, remember that when the snow melts, you might be walking on the defecation. In other words, for the safety of your shoes, if you have plans to be in the same yard area, you may want to set a specific rule.

1. Start by taking your puppy out each hour.
2. Go with your puppy.
3. Call his/her name and have him follow you.

4. If your puppy tries to pee or defecate in an area you do not want, pick him/her up and carry the puppy to the location you want.

5. After the first successful potty time, walk your puppy to the same area of the yard each time. Allow your puppy to sniff the area and remember this is his/her allowed location.

You may not care where in the yard your puppy goes, but you want it to be the same each time. For this, you can let your puppy pick a spot. After that spot is picked, then you can bring your puppy to that location each time he/she needs to go. Always pick him/her up if the puppy does not return to the same spot.

Let your puppy sniff the old spot.

If your puppy has learned commands, it will be easier; however, most will need to be taught outside toileting rules before they are old enough to learn the voice commands.

Never yell.

Never say "no."

Just be calm, pick up your puppy and place them on the spot they should go. If the matter is urgent, your puppy will immediately be set down and go to the bathroom.

Repetition will ensure follow through.

What to do if your Puppy is not listening

There is a chance that your puppy will not come when called, will not sit or stay, and follow the rule of going to the bathroom in a specific location.

It means you need to provide more training with a reward they want.

Your puppy likes praise, treats, and feeling comfortable.

You may need to start off with treats; particularly, if there is an issue with listening.

Take your puppy to the right location.

Let him/her sniff around.

If she/he goes to the bathroom, provide a treat.

Next time, take your puppy to the right spot.

If he/she tries to go elsewhere and succeeds before you can stop him/her, do not provide a treat.

Only when the right location is used, will you provide a treat.

You always want to reward good behavior, ignore the bad, and certainly never yell.

It might take several tries, but after your puppy learns there is something good waiting with the right toileting spot, the puppy will be more inclined to listen.

Chapter 6: Clicker Training

Clicker training is one method you can use to train your dog regarding voice commands, such as sit, stay, lay down, and walk.

What is it?

There is a device, invented in the 1900s that makes a clicking noise dogs can hear. The idea is to provide a voice command, along with a click, quickly followed by a treat when you see the response you want.

The Benefits

Your dog will learn your voice and your leadership; however, most people find it beneficial to train via associative learning techniques. This goes back to Pavlov, where you have a stimulus that elicits a response and then you can introduce something else to get that same response. It will stop your dog from being dependent on treats, as well as save your voice from needing to yell to call your puppy. The clicker can be heard over a long distance.

How to do it

You will need to start off with a behavior you want to train.

Associate this behavior with a treat, for example, "sit."

Tell your dog to sit.

You will need to raise your hand, up, with the treat in it.

The treat will be high and over their head, so when they look at the treat in your hand, their bottom plops on the floor.

Immediately give the treat.

Next, say sit. Raise your hand and when they sit, give them the treat.

After the repetition of saying sit and putting them into a position that they sit; thereby, getting a treat, they will know to sit just by your voice.

You can start to vary the praise, such as treats, a good rub down, or the word "good."

You have to associate, the movement and often show the puppy what you want by forcing their body into the natural position. It will take time because your puppy may try to jump. Jumping won't get a reward, but sitting will.

Once this correlation is made, you can start to introduce the clicker.

Provide a command, such as sit. Sound the clicker and give a treat.

Now your dog, knows you asked him/her to sit and got a treat, but there was a new noise.

Next, ask for your dog to sit, when you sound the clicker. If your dog sits, give him a treat.

Drop the word sit, but hold the clicker and treat over his/her head.

Again, you are placing your dog in a position to look up and naturally sit.

When the sound of the clicker is made, the dog will sit and get a treat.

After a few times repeating the clicking noise, and getting the dog to sit, you can avoid using the words.

You can also vary the reward from treats to praise.

You never want to train the dog that the clicker is simply to get his attention. Rather, you want the puppy to realize, you are asking him/her to do something, and when he/she fulfills the request, there is a reward.

Methods for Teaching Commands

Here are the steps for different commands:

Sit

1. Raise your hand, so the puppy follows the movement.
2. Just before your puppy plops his bottom, sound the clicker.
3. Give a treat.
4. Repeat the process.
5. Make sure you sound the clicker before your puppy sits.
6. After your puppy sits, successfully, with the clicker slightly above his/her head, lower your hands and make the clicking sound.
7. If your puppy sits, the puppy gets a reward.
8. If the puppy does not, raise your hand a little higher and try again. Until the puppy sits.

Basically, as you teach the clicker, lower your hand a little bit at a time, so that the natural position of the head back and bottom plopping on the floor becomes associated with the noise and not where your puppy is looking.

After your puppy sits, with the clicker at eye level or in your lap, you can move your hands behind your back. In this way, the puppy will associate the noise and not hand movements.

As always, provide a reward when your puppy sits following the clicker noise.

If you need to go slowly. Some dogs learn at a slower pace. Keep being consistent and repeating the good behavior. Ignore the bad behavior. If your dog is not listening, wait and try again. You need to have your puppy's attention.

There will be times when your puppy is stubborn. He/she may be too excited or wanting to play. For training, you need an obedient puppy, one that is not rowdy or excited. Let your puppy calm down, get a few minutes' rest, and then ask your puppy to try again.

Stay and Lay Down

The same procedures can be used for other commands. However, you need to have a different click. Since you are not using voice commands, your puppy will not know what you want. Of course, you can also train with voice and clicker commands, so your puppy associates the words and click with a command.

Most owners like to use a click only. If this is the case, then for "sit," you may have one click. For "stay," you will have two rapid clicks. For "lay down," you can have two slow clicks or three rapid clicks.

Again, you want your puppy to associate the behavior with the click. So, give the click order you want and reward for the good response. Ignore the inappropriate responses.

Give your puppy a break if he/she is not listening and then try again. Always, wait for the bad behavior to end, by being calm and ignoring it, and rewarding for the appropriate response.

As with sit, you want to provide the natural position with "stay" and "lay down."

Holding the clicker above the head a little longer for "stay" is one way to make your intentions clear. Your puppy will continue to look up and naturally stay in the position, in order to get the treat.

Do not wait too long or your puppy will think there is no reward and not follow any command. A few beats will be all you want to wait.

Chapter 7: Crate Training

Crate training can be beneficial for anyone who needs to leave the house for any length of time. It is also helpful for those who do not wish to sleep with their dogs during the night.

What is Crate Training?

Crate training is a process, where you teach your puppy that the crate is not a place for punishment, but a safe, familiar location. Many dog experts believe a crate can symbolize a den or cave dwelling to your dog, which is considered a safe haven in the wild. Your dog has the natural instincts to hide from danger during sleep, as well as a raise a family, so you want the crate to symbolize this.

The Benefits

- Your dog has some place to sleep
- You do not have to allow your puppy to sleep on your bed
- You can use it to house train
- It can be a safe place for your dog, whether you are home or not

How to do it?

Start by introducing the crate in a casual manner.

You do not want to bring your puppy home and lock him/her inside the crate immediately.

Make the crate seem like another piece of furniture, with a blanket, a few toys, and make sure the door will remain open.

Leave the area.

Your puppy will use his natural curiosity to examine the crate.

Do not immediately close the crate door, if your puppy goes in to investigate it.

Let your puppy sniff, explore, and enter at their own will.

It will teach your puppy that it is not a place to be feared.

If your puppy is not immediately interested that is okay. Have the crate somewhere you might spend time, so they get used to it being around.

After a while your puppy will get curious, particularly, if you are not paying attention.

Let your puppy start associating the crate with meal time; especially, if you are going to be out of the house for eight hours a day working.

Your puppy will have to learn how to eat and drink, without defecating in the place they will be all day.

Your puppy does not want to sleep in the same place it goes to the bathroom, so he/she will try to control their bladder.

After your puppy has explored the crate and feels more comfortable with it, you can close the crate door. It is a good idea to do this at meal time.

Put food in the crate, and when he/she is done eating open the door. Each time it is time for a meal, let your puppy remain inside a little longer. After a while, your puppy will get used to the idea.

It is also possible that your puppy will start to whine. This is fine. Go about your business, and show your puppy that the whining, barking, or shrill behavior is not going to get him/her out of the crate. You want the whining to stop before you open the door.

If you go to the door and open immediately, your puppy will associate whining with an open door. This will be bad when you have to leave for the day.

You do not want to create stress either. You will need to be slow about increasing the time your puppy stays inside the crate. If he/she whines the first time you close the door, wait, and open the door. Not long, just enough to show that you are not rushing to the crate to open the door at their command.

Methods of Getting Your Dog into the Crate

Toys, blankets, treats, and food are four methods of getting your dog into his crate. These can become bribery methods, so you want to make certain you are not rewarding hesitant behavior.

You do want to show him/her that the crate is a friendly, safe place to be.

Each time you put your puppy in the crate, use either a toy, treats, or food. For the first few days. You will then start to vary it. One time, you call your puppy's name and if the puppy goes in, you give him/her praise. After the praise, you might give a toy. The idea is you must vary the reward, so your puppy does not refuse to go in the crate when you call his/her name.

How Long Your Dog Should Spend There?

The amount of time your puppy remains inside the crate is dependent on a couple of factors. First, how old is the puppy? If you have a month old puppy, he/she will need to be let out nearly every hour to go to the bathroom.

As your puppy becomes older, you can extend the time.

The time extended in the crate should be associated with you gone from the house or during the sleeping hours.

If you close the crate when you are home, it will seem like a punishment. The idea of the crate is to provide a safe place, but also a place they can be when you are gone.

Most puppies will get into their crate when the door is open, take a nap, and be happy. Of course, it doesn't happen every time and it usually depends on whether they are tired of other places.

Also note that a lot of the time, your puppy will get into his/her crate when feeling poorly, insecure, or stress if they associate it with a safe place.

For example, an individual had a bear break in their house because they live near a national park. The dog and the owner were home at the time. The dog would hear noises and bark at near everything, alerting to possible danger. Yet, several times this same dog also slept in his crate instead of out in the living area. The dog felt safer in the crate due to fear and the smell of the bear in other areas of the house.

Crating at Night Time

Crating at night time is a routine like any other part of the day.

You want your puppy to associate your movements with sleeping in the crate.

It can be joyous to have a dog sleeping beside you, but let's face it, they are bed hogs.

You need to start from day one, letting your puppy know he/she will not be sleeping with you.

You need to make it clear that when the TV goes off and it is the appropriate bed hour, your puppy goes in his/her crate.

Your puppy may whine.

This is the time to ignore it, be quiet, calm, and if necessary keep the lights on low.

Your puppy will associate the quietness, with bedtime, and stop whining.

You can provide rewards, such as praise or treats the first few times, but always call their name, make sure they are inside, and close the door before giving a treat.

If your puppy continues to whine, you may need to provide a room, with no stimulation or things they can destroy. Close the door. Leave the crate open. Your puppy will start associating the routine. Most likely they will go into the crate and sleep.

Sometimes puppies just want the offer of freedom, so being able to go in and out of the crate at night time can be useful.

If this is the case, have a place where they can relieve themselves, provide no toys, and nothing that they will destroy, due to boredom.

Chapter 8: How to Walk Your Puppy

You had to learn how to crawl before you could walk and before you could run. Your puppy has stages they need to go through to understand how to walk on a leash properly. Just as you were at a young age, your puppy is unaware of certain dangers and how to contain their excitement.

Your puppy thinks, "Yay, I get to go outside." On a leash, he/she is thinking, but what is this horrible thing keeping me from running wherever I want to go. You will need to take small training steps to help your puppy learn how to go on walks with you, with or without a leash.

How an Untrained Puppy Acts?

An untrained puppy is unaware of the dangers. You have to show your puppy that there is danger and that you are going to protect them.

At first, on a leash, your puppy is going to strain against the new resistance they are subjected to.

Your puppy is going to jump, buck, and otherwise move around trying to get out of the collar/harness and leash.

If you are in a new place to teach your puppy how to walk on a leash, they are going to want to smell everything. Their sense of smell tells them all sorts of information, such as if something is good, bad, or interesting. It also tells them if another animal has been around.

Your puppy will run from one side of the walkway to another.

They will forget about the leash and wrap around you in their excitement.

Most puppies also try to run ahead and pull you with them.

How to Teach Walking Properly

To teach walking properly to your dog, you must first practice in an area they are familiar with.

Start by putting the collar or harness on your puppy.

Let your puppy walk around the house with the item on. Your puppy needs to become familiar with how the collar or harness feels, before you add new elements to the situation.

When your puppy stops trying to wiggle out of the harness/collar, stops chewing on it, or trying to pull it off with their teeth, you are ready for the next step.

Putting on the Harness or Collar

1. Ask your puppy to sit
2. Reward the proper behavior
3. Ask your puppy to stay
4. Reward the proper behavior
5. Hold the harness/collar in your hand and let your dog smell it.
6. If your dog tries to bite it, calmly say "no" or your command that usually requests your puppy stop their current behavior.

7. After your dog inspects the harness/collar, and understands it is not a toy, move to put it on.

8. Your dog might resist. If there is resistance, move the harness/collar back in your lap, repeat the sit and stay commands, and let your dog smell the collar again. Also slow your movements.

9. When you get the first clip on the harness/collar in place, pet your puppy in his/her favorite place. This is the reward for letting you get the harness in place.

10. Let your puppy walk around with the harness/collar on.

11. Repeat these steps, until your dog becomes comfortable with the feel of the harness.

12. Every day for a week, repeat the steps.

Adding the Leash

13. Put the harness/collar on.

14. Ask your puppy to stay, instead of letting him/her get up and walk round or play.

15. Hold the leash in your hands. Bundle it up, so it is in one hand.

16. Let your puppy smell the leash.

17. When your puppy shows disinterest, clip the leash in place.

18. Stand up and hold the end of the leash.

19. Indicate to your dog that he/she may walk.

20. When they reach the end of the leash, they will stop, turn, and look at you. They may also feel the leash on their back or around their legs. Your puppy will look at you. Let your puppy feel the leash and the stopping sensations.

21. When your puppy reaches the end of the leash or gets tangled, ask your puppy to sit and stay. Your puppy will associate your commands and the feel of the leash, with proper behavior.

22. Repeat these steps as necessary.

23. After the sit and stay commands are learned on the leash, it is time to teach the walk command. You can do this with a clicker, voice, or touch.

24. Walk to your puppy. Have him/her sit and stay if they stood up.

25. Say walk and start walking.

26. Give your puppy a treat if they start walking in the same direction as you.

27. Ask your puppy to sit and stay again. Praise them for the behavior.

28. Say walk, and start walking again. Repeat, until the word walk is associated with your movement. You may also want to use a hand, such as a pat on their side to indicate they can walk too.

29. To stop your puppy or settle them down ask for the sit and stay commands.

30. Repeat and reward as necessary.

Above all, you want to be in a controlled environment when training on the leash. You also need your puppy to be in a training mood, meaning not excited or ready to play. Inside the house will work for the first few weeks of getting your puppy used to the feel of the harness and leash. It is also an environment where they know you ask for sit and stay as proper behavior when they are exuberant.

Taking Your Dog for a Walk

Walking your dog for the first time, should be around your home, where you usually let them run. They will associate you going outside and holding the leash with proper behavior, eventually.

For the first time:

1. Ask your puppy to sit and stay by the door.
2. Put the harness and leash on.
3. Open the door.
4. When your puppy reaches the end of the leash, ask for him/her to sit and stay.
5. Ignore improper behavior.
6. Wait a few moments.
7. Try again.
8. When the puppy follows your command, give him/her praise and a treat, just like you do during all training.
9. Use your walk command that you taught inside.
10. Provide a treat when your puppy follows the command.

11. If your puppy becomes too exuberant, rather than pulling or shortening the leash, try the sit and stay commands, just like you did inside.

12. Walk beside your dog several times around the enclosure. Let your dog smell things, go to the bathroom, and have fun, but maintain your position as the leader by using sit, stay, and walk.

13. Repeat this outdoor experience as necessary, with proper rewards.

Your puppy will associate the harness and leash with walks with you. When the commands are followed and you feel your puppy has been trained, go outside the area you usually allow your dog to roam free in. Show them that you still require the same behavior in a new area.

As your puppy learns to walk outside their usual boundaries, you can add new commands. These can be leash commands, where your puppy starts associating certain movements with the feel of the leash.

For example, if the leash is on the left, against their skin, you want them to turn left. If it is on the right, you want them to turn right. If the leash is above them, you want them to walk straight.

If you do not want to use the leash, you can use your hands for signals. Once you have trained different signals such as turn left, right, walk forward, or go home, you are ready to take your puppy out to dog parks, trails, and other fun places.

What to do if your Puppy pulls/sees another Dog

Each new adventure will bring excitement. If your puppy sees another person or dog, they may want to rush right up. Your puppy may also forget the commands you taught during a regular walk.

You need to remind your puppy that you are in charge. You are the leader of the pack.

First, tighten up the leash by shortening it.

This will bring your puppy right next to you.

It gives them less ability to jump or try to pull you towards the person or other dog.

They will also feel you, since you are so close.

Instead of continuing to walk, ask your puppy to sit.

Repeat the command and give him/her a gentle reminder of what you want, based on how you taught him/her to sit.

Ask your puppy to stay. Reward for followed commands.

Keep your puppy sitting and staying in the same position, as the other dog or person approaches. Give a reassuring pat or pet him/her.

When the other puppy or person is close, let the other owner determine if their dog will approach your good puppy.

Since excitement can be a factor, you will have to reinforce good behavior with plenty of praise, perhaps even a treat. It may take several tries to get your puppy to stop jumping, barking, or acting a little crazy in their attempt to see and approach another puppy. However, with a calm demeanor, repetition, and a big enough reward for good behavior your puppy will learn.

Treats and Walks

You definitely want to have treats along on your walk. There will be plenty of times where "good" and petting are sufficient, but for those really exciting times, when your dog listens and behaves, you want to have treats.

As with all training, food is a powerful motivator. Make sure you change where you keep the treats each time you walk. You do not want your puppy to know you are going for a treat.

How Long Should you go on a Walk with your Puppy

Walking your puppy will be based on several factors:

- Is it warm?
- What is their stamina?
- How long do you want to walk?

The temperature will be a factor. Cold temperatures mean cold puppies. Hot temperatures can mean your puppy needs lots of water for a long walk. You do not want to dehydrate your puppy.

All puppies have different stamina based on breeds. Short legs, and fat bodies will require less walking. Bigger breeds, known for their endurance may need an hour's walk just to reduce their energy level. Read up about your dog breed to know how long to walk your puppy.

The distance is also based on you. How long can you walk for? How long are you willing to walk? You are the leader, so a walk is dependent on your stamina, as well.

Making your Puppy Sit Before Crossing a Road

One of the reasons you have taught your puppy to sit, stay, and walk with you, is road crossings. You do not want your puppy to be so excited about walking that they enter into dangerous situations.

Anytime you come to a road crossing it is important to ask your puppy to sit and stay, before giving the command to walk.

Your puppy will learn to associate cars and road crossings, with patience and your command. This way, even if your puppy gets off the leash, they will sit and not cross the road.

The more you train your puppy and work on their natural instincts to chase small animals or other puppies, the easier it will be to feel safe when your puppy is outside.

You can also start walking with your puppy off the leash, after enough time on the leash has occurred. However, you should do so in a controlled environment like a park or forest. In this type of environment, you get to teach your dog to sit, stay, and walk beside you even off the leash.

It will take time. As you walk on the leash, you will give more and more leash to your puppy, so when you make commands it is not at the end of the leash, but at any time.

It is going to be a slow process. You will have to repeat the steps many times. In the end, you will have a well-trained puppy, capable of following your voice commands, even in excited times.

Chapter 9: Jumping and Biting

Young puppies, exuberant puppies, and just puppy behavior in general can lead to jumping and biting behaviors. You will not want your puppy to jump or bite, but what can you do? You can start training your puppy early on that jumping and biting are not acceptable. The first thing, you have to do as the owner, is teach all other people in your household and visitors that jumping and biting are not acceptable in your home. It is a matter of consistency for your dog, as he/she will learn that it is not a good behavior in any circumstance.

What is Jumping

Jumping can take on many forms. Your puppy may jump against you to get your attention. Your puppy might jump on and put his/her front legs against a door. Your puppy might jump onto furniture or other surfaces where he/she does not belong. Jumping when in a training course, such as jumping up onto a board that forms a tent, where they walk up and then down another side, is acceptable. Jumping can also be all four feet coming off the ground in excitement. Most individuals do not want their puppy to jump on them, on furniture, or against doors.

Understanding the Behavior

Jumping is caused by desire or need. Puppies who jump when you first walk in the door, desire your attention. Puppies who jump at doors may need to relieve themselves. Excitement is the most common reason puppies jump on people. Comfort is their desire when they jump on furniture, or jump on a door to try to get it open.

Typically, excitement occurs when you have been gone or out of the room. For example, if you have been asleep in one room and your puppy has been in their room, they may want to jump on you each morning. When you return home, your puppy may try to jump.

You always need to ask for proper behavior before giving anything to your puppy. If they are excited to see you and need to relieve themselves, you will not be doing yourself any favors, if you let them outside right away.

They learn quickly that if they jump and you open the door that they get part or all of what they want or need. It is better to ignore the improper behavior.

What to do to Solve It

1. Determine the reason for the behavior. If it is excitement or jumping at the door, it will be fairly evident.
2. Do not react to the behavior.
3. Ask your puppy to sit.
4. If your puppy refuses to sit, wait.
5. Do not make eye contact.
6. Go about your tasks, ignoring the behavior.
7. If necessary, because your puppy is jumping on you, turn away or use a knee to push your puppy back. Normally, you wouldn't want to touch your puppy at all; however, if your puppy is hurting

you, near to knocking you over, or otherwise making you unsteady, you have to let your puppy know it is not appropriate.

8. Once you are able, walk away and go about your business.

9. When your puppy is on all fours again, try the sit command.

10. Be calm.

11. Do not raise your voice.

If you react with excitement, this is an indication that your puppy can react with excitement.

If your puppy still refuses to sit on command, but is on all fours, do not praise him/her. Do not say hello. Continue with what you need to do. After, a short time, try the sit command again. Your puppy will realize that unless he/she sits, you are not going to greet him/her.

As soon as your puppy listens to the sit command, you may say "hello" in a calm tone. Calming reach down and pet your puppy. Shower him/her with a little love and affection. Always maintain your calm demeanor. The more excited you are, the more excited your puppy will be and there is a chance he/she will try to stand up or jump on you again.

There is every possibility that your puppy in excitement or need will continue to jump. You need to realize that excitement is an instinct. Your puppy does not think there is anything wrong in showering you with affection. Obviously, you want that affection. However, you have to show your puppy, there is a right and wrong way to get affection.

Rewarding the excitement, even when your puppy is on all fours, teaches them they can be so excited that they can knock you down. Rather, you want to show them that excitement is wonderful, as long as they are calm.

What is Biting

Biting can be shown in various forms. However, a strict definition is any act of using their teeth on anything that you deem inappropriate. Biting can occur on your furniture and other items because your puppy has a need to chew. Biting can also be used on you. Your puppy might nip you in play. They may bite harder by accident or they may bite because they do not know the behavior is wrong.

Understanding the Behavior

Puppies learn to bite for different reasons. One is instinct. There is an instinct for most dogs to chase small animals, such as rodents and kill for food. It is an ingrained, genetic instinct that domestic dogs have never lost.

Nipping may be done on clothes or your skin. Nipping to get your attention is a common tendency among certain dog breeds. Nipping in the form of play is also common with some dogs. Sibling dogs learn to play and defend themselves by biting. A nip is a soft bite that usually does not damage the skin. Biting will usually be hard and hurt.

You have to recognize that excitement, attention-seeking, play, and defense are all instinctual behaviors that you have to train around, when it comes to biting.

What to do to Solve It

You are naturally going to have a reaction to being bitten; especially, if it is hard enough to hurt.

Saying "ouch" is an appropriate reaction. You can also whimper in pain. You want your puppy to know that you were hurt.

Your dog will not want to hurt you. If you say "ouch" and move your hand slowly away, your dog will associate the word and movement.

You do not want to yell or cause the puppy harm in return.

Your puppy will either think you are playing too or they will learn to associate you with abuse.

Play Nipping

1. Slowly move your hand.
2. Put your hand in a place your puppy cannot nip again.
3. Ask your puppy to sit.
4. If your puppy is already sitting, use the "stop" command.
5. Hand your puppy a toy.

During play, you want your puppy to associate their nipping behavior as incorrect, but you do not want to punish. When your puppy has sat down or calmed down, you want to reward your puppy. A toy they can chew will also help distract your puppy. If the mouth is busy with a toy, it cannot nip you.

However, you need to wait until the puppy is calmer. You do not want to associate the nipping with an immediate toy.

This is where many owners get into trouble. The dog nips, so the person reaches for a toy and says "here entertain yourself." The next time, the puppy comes up, nips and gets a toy. If this process is repeated, the puppy learns they get a toy every time they nip you. It is certainly not a good thing right?

Biting with Force

When biting is not part of play, but a misunderstanding that biting is acceptable, you have to teach your puppy it is not.

Again, you need to react calmly, without anger.

First, try to ignore the behavior.

If you need medical attention due to broken skin, calmly move to the area you keep this stuff stored and bandage yourself.

Above all, you do not want to give your dog attention.

If your puppy tries to bite you again or these incidents keep happening, you can try to whimper. Associate the pain you receive in a way your puppy will understand.

Once you made it clear you were hurt, ignore your puppy.

In a few moments, give your puppy a toy they can chew on.

Aggression and Biting

Outside of play, there are instances when your puppy might show aggression.

Early socialization is key. Animals that are socialized, learn how to behave properly in front of all people and other animals.

To decrease aggression, you will want your puppy to be spayed or neutered. Maturing puppies are more aggressive.

Next, do not allow playing biting of your appendages or clothing. Play biting of your person leads to more aggression.

Whimper, ouch, or ignoring the behavior is the first step.

If your puppy tries again to bite, take him/her to an area of time out. It does not mean you let him/her roam outside or show your puppy that the crate is punishment. Put him in a place without something he/she can get into, until your puppy calms down.

If these natural methods do not work, you can try store products that taste bad.

One option is a product called Bitter Apple. Dogs do not like the flavor. If you go to where you normally are when your dog bites, spray some on, and your pup tries to bite, he/she will be surprised. They will learn that the hand tastes awful.

Final Tips for Nipping/Biting

It will take time to get your puppy to stop biting. If you have shown him/her inappropriate behavior is allowed when he/she was young, it will take more time to correct the bad behavior.

Pushing your puppy away will make him/her think you are playing.

Letting your puppy nibble on your hand, will also teach him/her it is okay and the puppy may bite more, and harder the next time.

Associate anything like tug of war with play. Tug of war can be an aggression learned behavior for some dogs, where they start displaying more aggression. However, if you tug during play and give up when your puppy is too aggressive this will help.

If your dog's breed is naturally aggressive, it is best to avoid any sort of aggressive play.

Conclusion

Thank you again for purchasing this book!

I hope this book was able to help you with your puppy needs and to satisfy your reading pleasures.

You have done a great job reading through this book and now you have it as a guide for when you pick up your puppy. You can do anything you need to, in order to train your puppy correctly because you love your puppy already.

You want the best life for your puppy, as well as being content with his/her companionship. As long as you keep the reasons for getting your puppy in the forefront of your mind, you will succeed in training your beautiful new friend.

Your puppy is bound to make mistakes. There are no miracles in training your puppy. Just like it took you years to learn certain things, it will take your new friend time to learn, grow, and become an intelligent, mature dog. Be patient, walk away if you are frustrated, and remember every dog has a different learning curve.

Be consistent, be patient, and always be considerate of your new puppy's state of mind. You are the intelligent partner, who has already learned emotional control—now let your puppy learn from you.

Finally, if you enjoyed this book, please take the time to share your thoughts and post a review on Amazon. It would be greatly appreciated!

Thank you and good luck!

Made in the USA
Middletown, DE
23 January 2018